ROSANNE KELLER
LifeStories 1

New Readers Press

LifeStories 1
ISBN 978-1-56420-402-8

Copyright © 2003 New Readers Press
New Readers Press
Publishing Division of ProLiteracy Worldwide
1320 Jamesville Avenue, Syracuse, New York 13210
www.newreaderspress.com

Printed in the United States of America
9 8 7 6 5 4 3 2

All proceeds from the sale of New Readers Press materials support literacy programs in the United States and worldwide.

Acquisitions Editor: Paula Schlusberg
Content Editor: Terrie Lipke
Copy Editor: Marcia Hough
Production Director: Heather Witt
Designer: Kimbrly Koennecke
Illustrations: Linda Tiff
Production Specialists: Alexander Jones, Jeffrey R. Smith
Cover Design: Andrea Woodbury

Contents

Unit 1 Something Is Missing 5
       The Hunt 6
       Making Phone Calls 7
       Good News 8

Unit 2 Little Girls 9
       Children 10
       Neighbors 11
       Being Single 12

Unit 3 Calling New York 13
       Saturday Morning 14
       Time Zones 15

Unit 4 It's a Boy! 16
       Visiting the Hospital 17
       Dreams 18

Unit 5 Mixed Feelings 19
       Michael's Report Card 20
       Jealousy 21

Unit 6 Dinner Time 22
       Coffee or Tea? 23
       Whose Things Are Whose? 24

Unit 7 Carol's Job 25
What Can I Do? 27

Unit 8 May's Gift 29
A Bicycle for David 31

Unit 9 The Rocking Chair 33
Fred Gets the Flu 35

Unit 10 The Accident 37
Dream Store 39

Unit 11 Thanksgiving at 127 Center Street . .41
A Day for Thanks 43

Unit 12 Kendra's Family 45
Yes, I Can! 47

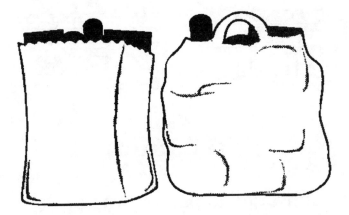

Something Is Missing

Carol goes shopping.

She goes to the supermarket.
She goes to the drugstore.
She goes to the bank.

Carol is glad to get home.
Then Carol says, "Oh no!"

Fred asks, "What is wrong?"

Carol says, "I do not have my purse.
What am I going to do?"

The Hunt

Fred and Carol look everywhere.
They do not find Carol's purse.

Fred tells Michael to go to the bank.
He sends Kendra to the supermarket.

Fred says, "I can go to the drugstore.
Don't worry, Carol.
We will find your purse."

"Wait!" Carol says.
"Don't go anywhere.
I can call on the phone."

Making Phone Calls

Carol looks up phone numbers.
She looks in the yellow pages.
She calls the bank.
Her purse is not there.

Carol looks up drugstores.
She calls the one on South Street.
Her purse is not there.

Carol calls the bank.
The bank is closed.
"What can I do now?" Carol asks.

"You can call the police," Fred says.
"Maybe they can help."

Good News

Carol is going to call the police.
But the phone rings.
Carol answers the phone, "Hello?"

Anita says, "Hi, Carol, this is Anita."
Carol tells Anita about her purse.

Anita laughs.
She says, "I am calling about your purse.
I am in the hallway.
I see your purse on the floor.
It is near your mailbox."

"I remember now!" says Carol.
"Thank you for calling me."

Little Girls

Fred Wilson's wife is Carol.
Richard Stevens is married to Janet.
The husbands are not brothers.
But Carol and Janet are sisters.
Alma and Harold Jones are their parents.

Alma smiles at Carol and Janet.
They are grown women now.
Alma shakes her head.
She remembers them as little girls.
She misses those little girls.

Then Alma looks at Kendra.
Kendra is her grandchild.
Alma still has a little girl.
There will always be little girls.

Children

Janet is visiting Carol.
They sit on the front steps.
Both sisters are drinking coffee.
Janet wonders about Kendra and Michael.
She asks, "How are my niece and nephew?"

Carol says, "They are growing up fast!
But they are both fine."

Janet says, "Being a mother is hard.
But is it fun?"

Carol grins at Janet.
She says, "One day you will know."

Neighbors

The apartment house is a nice place.
All the neighbors share.
They share good times and bad times.
They help each other.

Carol is planning a party.
She wants to invite her neighbors.
She wants them to meet her family.

Anita is Carol's neighbor.
Carol invites Anita to the party.
Janet and Richard are visiting.
Carol wants Janet to meet Anita.

Carol invites everyone to the party.
Then she starts cooking.

Being Single

Janet and Richard Stevens are newlyweds.
They have not been married long.
They meet Anita at the party.
Anita likes Janet and Richard.
They look so happy.

Anita likes being single.
She eats when she is hungry.
She comes and goes when she wants.
Everything is just the way she likes it.

After the party Anita goes home.
She goes in and sits down.
Why does she feel so alone?

Calling New York

Anita dials 11 numbers.
She is calling long distance.
She is calling her nephew in New York.
Her nephew answers the phone.

Anita asks, "Arturo, how are you?"

Arturo answers, "I'm OK, I guess.
I miss my home in Mexico.
I miss my family."

Anita says, "I can fix that.
Why don't you visit me?
We are family, too.
We can cheer each other up.
I'll send you money for the bus."

UNITED STATES POSTAL MONEY ORDER			
00052736321	031109	60626	$ 25.00
SERIAL NUMBER	YEAR, MONTH, DAY	POST OFFICE	U.S. DOLLARS AND CENTS
PAY TO			
ADDRESS		FROM Anita Gómez	
		ADDRESS 127 Center St.	
USED FOR		Chicago, IL 60626	

⑆000008002⑆   00052736321⑈

Saturday Morning

Anita is writing letters.
She has to hurry.
The post office closes early today.

She writes to her family in Mexico.
She writes a note to her nephew, Arturo.
Then she walks to the post office.

Anita buys some stamps.
She needs special stamps for Mexico.

Then she buys a postal money order.
She makes it out to Arturo Soto.
She puts it in the envelope for Arturo.

Anita smiles as she walks home.

Time Zones

Janet and Richard are home in California.
Kendra wants to call her Aunt Janet.
Carol says, "It is too early.
It is only 6 A.M. in California."

Kendra frowns at her mother.
She says, "But it is after 8 o'clock!
I don't understand."

Carol gets an orange and a flashlight.
She shines the light on the orange.
She turns the orange in her hand.
She says, "The world turns like this.
The sunlight moves from east to west.
It is already morning here.
But the sun is not up in California."

Kendra says, "I understand now.
We talked about time zones in school."

It's a Boy!

Sonia is Anita's friend.
She has a new baby boy.
Anita is very excited.
She wants to go to the hospital.
She wants to see Sonia and her baby.

The hospital is a few miles away.
Anita decides to take the city bus.
The nearest bus stop is Sandburg Park.
The bus leaves there in 20 minutes.
Anita has a little time to buy flowers.
She will hurry.

Visiting the Hospital

Anita gets to the hospital.
She finds Sonia's room.
Sonia is holding her baby.

It is like a picture.
They are so beautiful.
Sonia looks so proud.
Her eyes are shining.
She smiles and looks at the baby.
Sonia cannot stop smiling.

Anita enjoys her visit.
Sonia lets her hold the baby.

Later, Anita takes the bus home.
She is thinking as she rides.
Someday she will have a baby of her own.
Anita cannot stop smiling.

Dreams

Tom Lin lives in the U.S. now.
In China, Tom lived in a small village.
People in the village walked everywhere.
There were very few cars.

In China, Tom walked everywhere, too.
He walked to school.
He walked to the store.
He walked to visit friends.
Tom wanted a bicycle.
His dream was to have a bicycle.

Tom is in Chicago now.
He rides a bus everywhere.
Now Tom's dream is to have a car.

Mixed Feelings

Fred works hard for his family.
He loves them.
He wants the best for his wife, Carol.
He wants everything for his children.

The children bring Fred great joy.
But they worry him, too.
And sometimes they make him angry.

Kendra is often loud and silly.
Her room is a mess.

Michael does not like to do homework.
Sometimes he gets bad grades.

Fred thinks about all this.
Children bring both joy and trouble.
Fred would not trade them for anything.

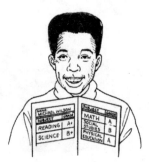

Michael's Report Card

Michael does not like school.
He wants to play baseball.
He wants to ride his bicycle.
He wants to watch TV.
Michael hates to go to school.

Then Michael gets a new teacher.
He likes this teacher very much.
He likes the way she talks.
He enjoys going to school now.
He works very hard.

His report card improves.
Michael gets all A's and B's.
Fred and Carol are so proud of him.
Michael feels great now.

Jealousy

Kendra hears her parents talking.
They tell Michael how proud they are.
They tell him he is a good boy.

Kendra always makes good grades.
Are they proud of her?
She thinks they like Michael more.
She feels angry and hurt.
She wants to hit Michael.

Kendra tells her mother she is angry.
Carol puts her arm around Kendra.
She says, "You are our best girl.
You were the first to make good grades.
Now Michael is doing well, too.
We can be proud of both of you.
You and Michael are both very smart."

Dinner Time

May is learning English.
She says, "English is a crazy language."

Tom says, "You can say that again!
I am, you are, he is. That is crazy."

May says, "It's hard to remember.
Is it *I does* or *I do*?"

Tom sighs, "Let's read your lesson.
Am I? Do I? Are you? Do you?
Is she? Does she? Is it? Does it?"

May says, "*I am. I do. You are. You do.*
She is. She does. It is. It does."

Tom says, "*I am* hungry.
Do you want to eat or just talk?"
Tom and May laugh.

Coffee or Tea?

Tom and May go to visit Fred and Carol.
They knock on the Wilsons' door.

Fred says, "Come in."

Tom asks, "Are you busy?"

Fred answers, "No. Come and join us.
We are just drinking coffee."

Carol says, "Fred has too much coffee.
He drinks it all day long.
With breakfast, he drinks coffee.
At work, he drinks coffee.
After dinner, he drinks coffee.
May I get you some coffee?"

Tom and May sit down.
Tom says, "I would like some coffee.
But May drinks only tea." Tom smiles.
"She drinks it all day long."

Whose Things Are Whose?

Kendra and Michael are bored.
It is raining.
They are tired of TV.
Michael starts to play a video game.

Kendra says, "That is *my* game!"

Michael yells, "It is not *yours*.
It is *mine*."
Then he says, "It is really *our* game.
Grandmother gave it to both of us."

Kendra yells, "She did not!"

Alma walks into the room.
"You need to share the game," she says.
"It belongs to both of you."

Kendra frowns at her grandmother.
She says, "I don't like this game.
Michael, it is yours now."

Carol's Job

Kendra and Michael are in school.
Fred is at work. Carol is home alone.
Anita calls on the phone.
"Carol, I have good news.
I will be getting more money now.
I got a raise at work."
Carol is happy for Anita.

Later Carol washes the dishes.
She makes the beds and sweeps the floor.

Then Carol stops and thinks.
I work hard, and *I* don't get a raise.
I don't even get paid!
The kids are in school all day.
I think I'll get a job.

Carol goes to the employment agency.
She talks to Mr. Willis.
He is the employment counselor.

Mr. Willis looks at Carol's forms.
He asks, "What kind of job do you want?
You once worked in a restaurant.
Do you want to be a cook?"

Carol laughs.
"No, I cook enough at home.
I was a cashier at the restaurant.
I enjoy working with people.
I think I'd like to work in a bank."

What Can I Do?

May Lin is lonely.
She stays home all day alone.
She would like to get a job.
But she did not go to high school.
May is trying to learn English.
But it is hard.

Lily asks, "What do you want to do?"

May says, "I want to be a teacher."

Lily says, "How can you be a teacher?
You did not go to college.
And you are just learning English."

May says, "Then what can I do?
I can only do housework or wash dishes."
May starts to cry.
"I do not have any experience.
But I want to work with children."

Lily says, "You don't have to be a teacher
to work with children.
Many parents work outside the home.
They need child care.
Maybe you can care for someone's child."

May says, "I would like that.
How can I find a job in child care?
Can I go to the employment agency?
I am afraid.
What will they think of me?"

Lily says, "They will like you, Mom.
They will see how nice you are.
They will want to help you."

May's Gift

Anita and Carol are talking. Anita says, "Next week is May's birthday."

Carol says, "We should buy her a present. Let's go shopping this weekend."

On Saturday, Anita and Carol walk down the street. They pass a pet store. There are puppies, kittens, fish, and birds for sale. Carol says, "We cannot have dogs or cats in our apartment house."

Anita says, "We can have a bird or a fish. Look, the birds are half price." They go in the door. The birds screech and sing loudly.

Carol says, "That noise would drive May crazy! Besides, even at half price, birds are expensive."

Anita says, "Look at the fish. We can buy May a goldfish. They do not cost much. And they are so pretty."

A sign says, "Goldfish: $3.75 each."

Anita and Carol agree to buy the goldfish. A fishbowl is $8.50. They also buy some fish food. With tax, the total comes to $15.82. Carol and Anita each pay half. Carol writes a check for $7.91. Anita pays her share in cash.

Anita carries the fish in a plastic bag. Carol carries the fishbowl and food. Carol says, "Now May will not be lonely. She will have a pet."

A Bicycle for David

May and Tom are walking in the park. Many people are riding bicycles. Tom says, "I want to buy a bicycle for David. There is a bike shop near here."

Tom and May go to the bicycle shop. They look at new bikes. They look at used bikes. The used bikes look just like new. Tom says, "Bikes that have been owned by someone else don't cost as much as new ones."

Tom looks and looks. The used bikes start at $89. Some of the new bikes cost hundreds of dollars. He looks only at the used ones. Then Tom sees a silver one. Tom asks, "How much is this bike?"

The salesman says, "This one is $95. It is on sale from $129."

Tom says, "I'll take it. And I want one of those helmets for $30." Tom smiles and gets out his wallet.

The salesman says, "With the tax, that comes to $132.50."

May looks at Tom. She sees his eyes shining. She remembers when they were children in China. Tom wanted a bicycle more than anything.

Tom says, "I think I'll ride it home. I want to check it out for David."

May just smiles. A bike for David? No. She sees her husband's dream come true.

The Rocking Chair

Kendra wakes up crying. She is holding her ear. She cries, "It hurts!"

Carol says, "The health center does not open until 8 o'clock. That is an hour from now."

Fred sits down in the big rocking chair. He says, "Come here, Kendra. Let me rock you until we go."

Kendra says, "I'm not a baby. I'm too big for that." She is holding her throat.

Fred tells her, "It's OK. Sometimes it helps to sit on your daddy's lap."

Kendra sits on Fred's lap. He puts his arms around her.

Fred says, "This old rocking chair helped you feel better many times. Do you remember when you fell off your tricycle?"

Kendra says, "I hurt my knee. But you rocked me, and I felt better."

Carol says, "When you were a tiny baby, you fell off the sofa. You got a bump on your head. We were so scared!"

Fred says, "I rocked you until the taxi came. Then we rushed you to the doctor." Fred laughs. "He said you were hard-headed! Nothing would hurt you." Fred looks at his watch. "It's time to go now."

Kendra says, "My ear still hurts. But I feel better now, Daddy. When I come home, can we rock some more?"

Fred Gets the Flu

Fred wakes up in the middle of the night. He feels hot. His throat hurts. His eyes burn. His head is pounding.

He gets up and looks in the mirror. His eyes are red. His nose is running. He is coughing. He looks terrible. He says, "Oh, no, I have Kendra's flu."

In the morning, Carol takes Fred to the health clinic. The doctor suggests a cough syrup for Fred's cough. He suggests aspirin for pain and fever.

Fred goes back to bed when he gets home. Carol puts his medicine on the bedside table. She says, "You can take the cough syrup four times a day. Take the aspirin every six hours for pain."

Fred asks, "Can I have coffee?"

Carol says, "Yes, but only one cup. Coffee keeps you awake. You need to rest to get well."

Later, Kendra and Michael come into the room. Kendra gets up on the bed. She puts her arm around her father. She says, "You are too big to rock, Daddy. But I can hold you. You are not too big to hold."

Fred leans against Kendra. He says, "My family is the only medicine I need."

The Accident

David Lin just got home from school. He is unlocking the door to his apartment. Just then he hears a terrible noise. He looks out the window. Two cars just crashed at the corner.

David runs to the corner. The drivers are still in their cars. One woman is crying.

David says, "I'll call for help." He takes out his cell phone. He calls 911.

He says, "There was an accident. Two cars crashed at the corner of South Street and Center Street. People are hurt."

Someone is helping one of the drivers. David goes over to the other car. He opens the door and sees a woman crying.

She asks David, "Is my baby OK? My seatbelt is stuck. I cannot get out."

David sees a crying baby in the back seat. He gets in the car. He sits next to the baby's car seat and talks to the baby. He holds the baby's hand.

Soon the baby calms down. Then the police and paramedics arrive. No one is badly hurt.

The woman thanks David for taking care of her baby. The police thank David for calling for help. David feels like a hero.

Dream Store

Tom Lin wants to own his own business. His friend tells him about an empty store for rent.

His friend says, "This space has three big rooms. It is in a nice neighborhood. The store closed a long time ago."

Tom goes to look at it. The empty store is very dirty. It needs cleaning. That would be a big job.

The electricity needs to be checked. Some windows are broken. The floors need new carpet. The checkout counter looks very old. It will have to be replaced.

Tom closes his eyes. He sees a bright, clean store. He sees the shelves full of boxes. He sees a computer on a new checkout counter. Tom sees shining glass windows in front. He sees himself opening the door to his own store.

Then Tom opens his eyes. He sees a big mess. Tom sighs. This place is not like his dream. He cannot afford to buy new things. The store would be too much work. And it would cost too much money.

So Tom's dream will have to wait.

Thanksgiving at
127 Center Street

It will soon be Thanksgiving Day. Carol is making a list. She is planning a surprise. She will fix a big Thanksgiving dinner.

Carol will invite everyone in the apartment house. She is going to invite Janet and Richard to come also. There will be 11 people for dinner. Thanksgiving will be a day to celebrate with her friends and family.

Kendra is excited. She is learning to cook. Carol says she can help.

Thanksgiving is a very American holiday. This will be a perfect Thanksgiving dinner. Carol and Kendra will roast a big turkey. They will make cornbread stuffing. They will mash potatoes. They will make gravy. They will fix cranberry sauce. And, of course, for dessert there will be pumpkin pie!

Then Kendra has an idea. She says, "Let's ask May and Lily to bring some Chinese food. And Anita can bring some Mexican food."

Carol says, "What a good idea! We can have an international Thanksgiving dinner!"

A Day for Thanks

Thanksgiving is a cold day. But everyone at 127 Center Street feels warm. Thanksgiving dinner is going to be at 2 o'clock in the afternoon. Everyone is cooking or getting ready.

May Lin is bringing fish and vegetable stir fry. She lays out everything she needs. She has vegetable oil, chopped ginger, oyster sauce, snow peas, onions, mushrooms, tomatoes, bell pepper, and fish. She is heating her wok.

Anita is bringing cheese enchiladas. She chops onion and garlic. She gets out chili powder, tomato puree, salt, and pepper. She has three kinds of cheese. She will mix everything together and then wrap it in tortillas.

Kendra is helping Carol roast the turkey. Carol made the stuffing. Kendra will mash the potatoes. Janet is baking pumpkin pies.

At 2 o'clock everyone is gathered around the table. The room smells wonderful. Fred stands up. He says, "I would like to give thanks for my family and friends this special day."

Then May stands up. She has been practicing her English. She says, "I am thankful for this food. But I am most thankful for my new American friends."

Kendra's Family

Kendra is doing homework. She has to make a report. She is going to report on her family.

Kendra writes: "I don't have a big family. I have a medium-size family. I have a mother and a father. I have a brother. I don't have a sister. I wish I had a sister. My brother doesn't have a brother. He really wants a brother.

"I have two grandmothers and one grandfather. My father doesn't have a father. My father's father died. So I only have one grandfather.

"I have an aunt. She is my mother's sister. She and my mother don't have a brother. But I do have an uncle. His name is Richard. He is married to my aunt.

"I wish I had a dog. But I don't. My family doesn't have a dog. Dogs are not allowed in our apartment. I wish I had a cat. If I had a cat, I would name it Alice. I like the name Alice.

"That is all about my family."

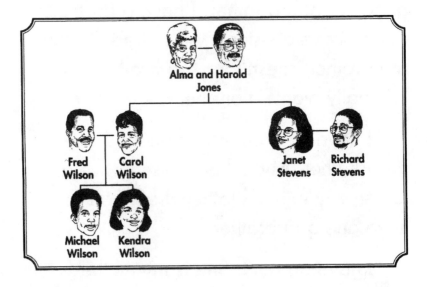

Yes, I Can!

May Lin takes English classes. She is having a hard time. One day she comes home from class. Tom asks, "How was your day?"

May starts to cry. "I can't do it!"

Tom asks, "Do what?"

May says, "I can't learn English."

Tom says, "May, you *can* learn English. You can! You can't do anything with *can't*. You have to start saying 'I can.'"

May says, "I went to the employment agency. I wanted to get a job. I want to take care of children. Lily said that is a job I can do. But the man said I have to speak better English. I have to speak English to the children. I can't do it."

Tom says, "Then we will do it. I will help you. Carol will help you. Even Kendra can help you. We have many friends. We can all help you practice your English every day."

May smiles. "And Anita can help me," she says.

Tom laughs. "Yes, Anita learned to speak English. And now she can help you learn, too."